INSTA-SUCCESS SYSTEM

Leverage Instagram to build your business, tell your story and dominate your competition!

Dylan Bradley

Copyright © 2017 Dylan Bradley

All rights reserved.

No part of this book can be reproduced by any form or by any electronic or mechanical means, including information storage and retrieval systems – except in the case of brief quotations in articles or reviews – with the permission in writing of its publisher, Dylan Bradley.

The information provided herein is stated to be truthful and consistent, in that any liability, in terms of inattention or otherwise, by any usage or abuse of any policies, processes, or directions contained within is the solitary responsibility of the recipient reader.

Please note the information contained in this book is for educational and entertainment purposes. Every attempt has been made to provide accurate, up to date and reliable information. No warranties of any kind are expressed, and readers acknowledge that the author is not engaging in the rendering of legal, financial, medical, or professional advice.

ISBN: 1542431603

ISBN-13: 978-1542431606

DEDICATION

This books is dedicated to my only sister, Shannon. For this reason, she is my favorite sister, and first on a long list of people that I dedicate my hard work to.

CONTENTS

ACKNOWLEDGEMENTS   i

Chapter 1   3

WHY USE INSTAGRAM FOR YOUR BUSINESS

Benefits of Starting To Build Now

Chapter 2   9

INSTAGRAM FEATURES

Start With The Basics

Chapter 3   13

TIPS ON HOW TO POST

So you don't look like every other fish in the sea

Chapter 4   17

THE BEST TYPES OF CONTENT

Master The Soft Sale

Chapter 5   25

WHAT NOT TO DO

Because Millennials Can Smell an Outsider from 10,000 Miles Away

Chapter 6   31

RESEARCH AND CHOOSE YOUR CATEGORIES

Wisely Damnit!

Chapter 7   35

RESEARCH TOP INFLUENCERS AND BRANDS

And You Will Eventually Become One of Them

Chapter 8   39

NOW FINISH YOUR ACCOUNT SETUP

So You Can Get To The Fun Part

Chapter 9   43

FINALIZE YOUR PROFILE THEME

Show The World Your True (Business) Self

Chapter 10   49

SECRET GROWTH STRATEGIES

That Most People Never Use

Chapter 11   63

BUSINESS CONTENT STRATEGIES

Putting It All Together

Chapter 12:   67

ANALYTICS AND METRICS

Turning Followers To ROI

Chapter 13:   73

ADVERTISING

The 2017 Way To Grow Your Business

Chapter 14: 81

CONCLUSION

Take. Action. Now.

Chapter 15: 83

RESOURCE SECTION

If You Don't Read Anything Else, This Is Your Section

Chapter 16: 89

THE SOCIAL SECRET

Skip This If You Are A "Millennial"

ACKNOWLEDGMENTS

Working on this book has been a process that I never could have completed all by myself. I'd like to thank the people who supported me throughout, including my immediate family,

Shannon, Conner, Isaac, Ethan, Steve, Robyn, and Mark. I could go into great detail about how my family has influenced my work on this project, but I think I would have to write another book. Simply put, they have been supportive of my every decision and never hesitate to throw their valuable two cents in.

Dad, you have always given me motivation to succeed in everything that I do, and I thank you for this. This book would have never surfaced if you had not pumped my brain with your sales content, and insisted that I utilize my Instagram as a business.

To Conner, for editing my mistakes throughout the process, making everything look nice, and adding a creative flare to the text. When I was lacking motivation, you provided the momentum and helped me get everything I needed done. I never thought I would depend on my little brother to design my book, but that day has indeed arrived.

CHAPTER 1

WHY USE INSTAGRAM FOR YOUR BUSINESS?

BENEFITS OF STARTING TO BUILD NOW

In a world where data is being produced and consumed at ever increasing rates, pictures truly are worth 1,000 words. In fact, analysts have estimated that each year the amount of new data created equals that of the total amount of data ever created.

If you haven't been paying attention, then you may be like everyone else – drowning in data but starving for information. If you haven't been using social media for business, then you may be part of the 80% of businesses that fail.

So why then, should you pay attention to Instagram when you already have Twitter and Facebook? The simple answer, because it's 2017, and Instagram is now one of the fastest growing social networks. The reason…Instagram is all about visual storytelling, and no other social network lets you showcase your story like Instagram.

Let's look at some data up front so you can see the main benefits of Instagram as well as some important stats on Instagram trends* (provided by The 2016 Social Media Examiner Industry Report).

- Instagram use by marketers jumped from *36%* in 2015 to *44%* in 2016.
- Marketers putting in 40 hours in a week are much more focused on Instagram compared to part time than any of the other platforms. 33% B2B & 51% B2C (Facebook, Twitter, LinkedIn, YouTube)
- 57% of marketers plan to increase their use of Instagram (63% B2C, 48% B2B).
- Only 12% of marketers use paid Instagram ads (potential opportunity).
- Most important content for marketers is: blogging 38%, visual 37%, videos 21%, live video 2% — and they want to increase video and visuals.
- There are over 500 million Instagram users and it is

growing! It has surpassed Twitter.
- Facebook - the most dominant media platform - owns Instagram.

Here are the top marketing benefits of using social media:

1. Increased exposure (89%) in as little as six hours a week.
2. Increased traffic (75%).
3. Developed loyal fans (68%); B2C gained more benefit than B2B.
4. Provided marketplace insight (66%).
5. Generated leads (66%) in as little as six hours a week.
6. Improved search rankings (58%).
7. Grown business partnerships (55%).
8. Established thought leadership (54%).
9. Improved sales (51%) in 11 to 40 hours.
10. Reduced marketing expenses (50%).

This book is designed to show you how to access those benefits for your business.

Not only is Instagram an investment in your current business but it is also a very important investment into the future success of your business. Given that Instagram is one of the most popular social media networks and it is owned by the most popular and powerful social media network in the world (Facebook) it is safe to assume it is here to stay.

If you're skeptical, consider the fact Instagram is a predominately mobile platform. We live in a time where mobile devices connect people and businesses on a global scale, and more people continue to use them. Simply put, the world is going mobile, and future of successful business will depend on how well that business can make the transition.

Consider that a lot of Instagram's current users are under 35. In a few short years, that population will age, and their spending habits will influence the marketing landscape tremendously. It is a very smart idea to connect with them now so that you will have their attention when things change.

As a business, you need to be where the people are in order to be seen and capture attention. If you fail to do this, then there is little hope that your business will be able to compete in the new digital landscape.

I put this book together so that you can start now and stay ahead of the game. In the following chapters, I will teach you how to leverage Instagram and convert consumer attention into sales. We will go through the fundamentals of success on Instagram, and you will leave with a head start on your competitors.

Dylan Bradley

CHAPTER 2

INSTAGRAM FEATURES

START WITH THE BASICS

Let's get started by reviewing the different features of the Instagram app so you can take full advantage of it.

Home Tab

This is the main tab where you get all the updates from the people you'll follow. You get to see their stories that they posted. You also can see the posts form your followers. These are shown to you in a feed based upon a combination of time (most recent on top) and relevance (determined by Instagram's algorithm). For your business account you probably won't use the feed very much. Since you need to focus more on your content and interacting with the people that interact with your posts (commenting back, visiting their profiles, etc…)

So your main use of the "Home Tab" is to create stories and setup Live videos, as well as review and respond to your direct messages.

Explore Tab

Use this tab to see what Instagram recommends for you. In addition, you can use it as a powerful search tool to find hashtags, different accounts, and posts by location. This is especially useful to connect with people in a certain area. Also use it to get ideas of things to post.

Camera Tab

The main feature of this tab is to upload your posts. This is important because Instagram makes you upload posts from the app. You can upload photos and videos. You can also take photos with the app, but I don't recommend this - more on this later.

News Tab

There are two main sections of this tab: "You" and "Following". In the "You" section you can see the notifications of who liked and/or commented on your posts and if you have anyone new following you.

To get to the "Following" tab, you can swipe to the side. In this tab you can see what your followers have liked, commented on, and/or started following. This is a good resource to get inspiration for your posts or find accounts to follow.

Profile Tab

This is where you can see all your posts, followings, followers, and tagged photos of you. This is also where you go to edit all your account settings and check all your analytics (only if you have a business profile). You can also switch between multiple accounts on this tab.

Dylan Bradley

CHAPTER 3

TIPS ON HOW TO POST

SO YOU DON'T LOOK LIKE EVERY OTHER FISH IN THE SEA

A quick list of tips for when you post, just to make sure you get off to the right start.

Don't be "Instant" with your posts

Don't take photos with the Instagram app and then edit them in the app that instant and post them. This will most likely lead to a post that does just about everything wrong if you are trying to have a consistent theme. You're a business, not a high school kid trying to show off a mirror selfie during lunch.

Do use the story feature for instant posts

The addition of the story feature on Instagram is the only time you should post what you are actually doing. It is quick, it will disappear in 24 hours, and it is a great tool to show you or your business in action. Post the pictures later after you edit them, caption them, hashtag them, and tag them - then use a story to make a call to action for people to view your photo.

Don't over edit

when you go to post in Instagram, you will get a bunch of photo editing tools. Do not go overboard with these. In fact I highly recommend editing your photos outside of Instagram for the best quality photos. However, you can use the in-app tools; just make sure you are consistent, but keep in mind this will take up more of your valuable time if you do it this way.

Do edit your photos

While you shouldn't over-edit or use the editing features in the Instagram app, you need to edit your photos. I recommend using an outside photo editing platform for these. If you're really serious about Instagram for business, I'd use a professional to edit your photos and ensure they are consistent with your company's Instagram theme.

Don't neglect your caption

The captions can make or break a photo. A great caption will drive more engagement than a bad one. There are a lot of different types of captions and methods. Just be consistent and don't over mention or over hashtag in your caption. This is where you mention the photographer, the event, or whatever the main mention is. Also just use one or two top hashtags here. You can do other mentions and hashtags elsewhere.

Do take advantage of all the options

You should have a caption, geotag your photo, tag relevant people/accounts (more on this later), and share to your connected social media sites. This will help maximize your engagement on your photo.

These were just a few tips for how to post. You will learn a lot more as you go through the rest of this book. Just know that if you fail to prepare, you prepare to fail. Be strategic and consistent with your Instagram account, and you will have no problem maintaining consistent growth.

Dylan Bradley

CHAPTER 4

TIPS BEST TYPES OF CONTENT

MASTER THE SOFT SALE

There are three main categories of Instagram content for you to be familiar with: <u>Posts</u>, <u>Stories</u>, and <u>Direct Messages</u>. There are subcategories in each of these, but your main focus should be to understand posts and then you can get more creative with the others.

Direct Messages

Anyone can send you a direct message. To be honest, if you're operating as a business a lot of the messages sent to you will be SPAM. You will get messages from followers that contain all sorts of "interesting" comments. With that being said, you shouldn't neglect this feature. Just review the messages you receive and some will be good to respond to. One of the best uses for your direct messages is to send notifications or offers to your followers (more on this in the growth hack section).

Stories

These are great and you should use them to showcase the live personality of your business. Do things like behind the scenes, show your products or business in action. Also you can pose questions and create calls to action to your followers here. A great strategy is to use a story to call out a recent post of yours in order to get more engagement. You want to try and get 5-6 story updates a day!

Posts

This will be your main content. So I am going to spend more time here and give you an overview of some of the top post types to maximize engagement. Keep in mind these will be in no particular order, and depending on your business some may be more beneficial than others.

Self Interest Posts

These speak to a specific benefit/want/need/desire that your audience has. These are great for frequent use because these will instantly connect with your target audience. These photos represent the main theme of your Instagram account.

Curiosity

These are posts that draw people in because they play on our natural curiosity. These are the "look twice" kind of posts that make your pictures stand out when they are in the photo feed.

I Need It

The goal of these posts is to make your audience want what you have. Think luxury items or scenes. Fancy food. Pictures doing business or meeting with celebrities. All of these things will trigger what I call an "I need it" response in people. Don't post too many of these because then you run the risk of looking like you just want to show off…unless that is what your brand is based on.

Exclusivity

Similar to the "I Need It" post but this just focuses on exclusivity. Like flying in a private jet, famous locations, attending fancy events, etc. The goal of these posts are to show you are doing well enough to command a level of exclusivity. If used correctly, these can put you in an authoritative position. Used incorrectly then you might just look like you have a huge ego (bad).

Humanity

Where the previous two posts tap into people's ego, this type of post triggers a heartfelt response. These are meant to show you are a human just like everyone else. Not perfect, just a person. Stories are great to show this, but also you can and should use this type of post and it can be one of the only "Instant" style posts because the whole point is not to be perfect.

Behind the Scenes

Too often your followers only see the finished product. This type of post does a great job showing what actually goes into making that finished product. Periodically posting this kind of content will
show your followers that what they see is only the tip of the iceberg

Reposts

A great way to drive a lot of engagement, but only if done correctly. Reposts share content that someone else has already posted. I recommend these for showcasing the work of similar brands or people that you aspire to be like. Or you can feature the posts of your followers to show them support and strengthen the relationship.

Crowdsourced Images

Similar to reposting, except these photos are more suited to show the winner of a contest you hold. You can ask your followers to take photos of any particular topic related to your business and then feature them later on (REI Example).

Quotes

Don't underestimate the power of sharing good vibes. These are great posts to spread out your content.

Ideal Visual Composition

These are the perfectly arranged items posts. They just look good. Everything is nice and neat and the underlying message is that you are organized and have great taste.

Influencer Images

Go out and connect with an influencer and have them take photos with your product or endorse your service. You will probably have to pay but it's a great way to spread the word and if you pick the influencer correctly, you will get great content to share. Think of it as a win/win.

Motivational Images

These are the typical mountain background with quote image. These are powerful. They show you doing something extraordinary. These show you in action on a level that connects with the hearts of your followers. You really can't stage this type of content. You have to live it.

Contests and Giveaways

Use these posts to get your followers engaged with your brand. Post an image with a caption announcing a contest or discounts on your products.

Show Me

Share how you do things. These are best done with short video clips. Step by step processes and things like that. Great for if you are a chef or fitness person.

Shoppable Posts

The whole point of these posts is to sell what is being featured. There are a lot of apps that you can integrate with for this, or you can just give a call to action in your caption and bio to get people to go to the link where you are selling what you just posted about.

Ask Your Followers

Use this type of post to get engagement from your followers. You literally ask them to help make a decision for you, provide feedback, or whatever you want. But it is a great way to show them you care about what they think and that they can actually contribute.

Lifestyle Shots

The point of these posts isn't anything to do with your business. These posts need to show how you live your life. They are great if your business allows you to have an awesome lifestyle. Think travel, events, activities, etc. All the things that you like to do - your hobbies. These are powerful because again they show you are just like everyone else, but also can show some exclusivity without being too "showy" with it.

So those are the main types of posts that you want to focus on to get maximum engagement. Obviously quality is always important. You don't need to use every type of post, but I recommend picking four or five "core post types" and then you can add in others here and there. This will ensure consistency and also allow you to spice things up when necessary. Also keep in mind that posts can fit into multiple categories and the type can change depending on your brand/business. In addition, the caption is very important in communicating the message behind the photos.

The biggest takeaway is that people follow you on Instagram for your story. They want to be able to relate to you. So you want to be able to communicate your story and your messages to your followers in a way that gets them to engage with your brand. The more you do this, the more quality followers you will have and the better return you will get on using Instagram for your business.

Dylan Bradley

CHAPTER 5

WHAT NOT TO DO

BECAUSE MILLENIALS CAN SMELL AN OUTSIDER FROM 10,000 MILES AWAY

The real secret to ensuring that you will have a successful Instagram strategy is to do your research first and build a strategy around that, but here are a few tips on what not to do.

Using the Wrong Research

You have to step outside your expectations when you conduct market research. Don't only study information that matches your assumptions, because you could be wrong. Even if you service or sell products to people you think are just like you and you're in your own target market, your experiences are subjective and not indicative of the experiences of others.

Avoiding Primary Research

Knowing the market size, how it's performing, and other information readily available to you is considered secondary research. And while it is good information, you need to also get information directly from your audience about your business. Being able to ask your target market directly about their thoughts, feelings, and actions can go far in helping you make good decisions.

Not Researching the Competition

Your competition is very important in your market research, because they likely sell to your audience. Knowing how they do things and whom they do it with, and everything else you can about how they do business, will help you do it just a little bit better. Differentiation is the key when it comes to winning against your competition.

Using Poor Reference Materials

It's important to understand what constitutes good research and what constitutes poor research. There are some legitimate places to research using the Internet and some that aren't. The best places to look are within scholarly research via university-approved publications. Be careful about using materials put out by propagandists.

Not Researching Your Audience

It's best to get access to a list of people who are definitely within your target audience. You can do this via list-building exercises, or you can locate your audience in your competition's groups and message boards. The more you can communicate with your audience directly and ask them the right questions, the better.

Using Out-of-Date Data

This is very important because even when the demographics stay the same, people change and grow with time. For example, the company Olay doesn't market their beauty products to their audience the same way today as they did in the 1980s. Their product really hasn't changed much, but they have to market to their demographic differently so they don't offend them. You should do the same and avoid using out-of-date information.

Not Using the Market Research

Believe it or not, many business owners don't even bother using any type of market research at all. They just stick with their assumptions and move forward. This is a huge mistake. When you conduct market research, you may confirm or completely defy your expectations.

Not Asking the Right Questions

When you start with market research, ensure that you're asking the right questions when you conduct surveys. Creating a good survey is a talent that can be learned. You must phrase the questions correctly, read about survey question mistakes, and learn how you can do better.

Remember that market research doesn't really ever end. Even when you complete the initial research, you'll need to continue with it throughout the lifetime of your business. Because, as mentioned before, even if you think your actual market demographics don't change, they do. They start using different technology, and their opinions and outlook on life evolve with every generation. Market research can help you keep up.

By monitoring the social channels, you use you can discover the answers to some very important sales and marketing questions such as:

- What does my target market care about?
- What are the most common "pain points" of those interested in my niche?
- What is trending in relation to my niche?
- What trends are driving sales?
- Who are my main competitors?
- How do my products compare or differ?
- What social media marketing efforts on their part might be worth imitating?

Now that you know what not to do and what kinds of things to look for in your market research read on to see how to do this research for Instagram!

Dylan Bradley

CHAPTER 6

RESEARCH AND CHOOSE YOUR CATEGORIES
WISELY DAMNIT!

Just like there are different categories of posts types, Instagram has different themed categories you can fall into. According to Iconosquare (a very useful Instagram analytics platform), there are 44 different categories that your account can fall under.

You will want to make sure that you fully understand he categories that apply to your business, so that you do not market to the wrong audience!

Check out the list below:

Instagram Categories			
Accessories	Fitness	Lingerie	Selfie
Adventure	Food	Mobile only	Shoes
Architecture	Gaming	Motorbike	Soccer
Automotive	Graphics	Music	Sports
Cats	Hairstyles	Nails	Tattoos
Cosmetics	Health	Nature	Technology
Design	Illustration	People	Travel
Dogs	Interior Design	Photography	Urban
Drinks	Kids	Quotes	Watches
Entertainment	Landscape	Reposts	Wedding
Fashion	Lifestyle	Science	Yoga

CHAPTER 7

RESEARCH TOP INFLUENCERS AND BRANDS:

AND YOU WILL EVENTUALLY BECOME ONE OF THEM

This is essential if you want to use Instagram for your business. You will want to figure out who is the best in your space. Research them and learn what they do, so you can do it and potentially improve upon it. Doing this is something that most businesses don't do and will automatically set you apart from the competition. You can get as granular as you want and do this research for each category you chose as well as each post type you plan on using. Then just make a list of the top influencers and brands and keep that handy.

I am going to briefly go over what data you need to collect and analyze for this research. Really quick, there are a lot of analytic software platforms out there. I like Iconosquare, but you can do this research in the Instagram app as well.

Here is what you need to collect:

- **Number of Posts and Post Types Used:** you can see if they are scheduling posts and if they have a particular system they use.
- **Number of Followers and Number of Followings:** ideas for accounts to follow and used to calculate engagement metrics.
- **Usernames** (for both future tagging and also branding ideas)
- **Profile Photos** (branding ideas)
- **Bio:** to give you an idea of how to structure your bio.
- **Links:** you should have a link in your bio, but this will show you how the link should look.
- **Tags:** look and see how many tags and who is being tagged by these accounts. Also see who is tagging these accounts.
- **Mentions:** these will be in the captions.
- **Captions:** there are different caption types; understand what the best are doing.
- **Engagement:** this metric you have to calculate, but it is simply the amount of likes/total followers. It can also be the

amount of comments/total followers. And you can combine those as well. Tip* comments are more valuable than just likes.

Don't underestimate the importance of doing this when you start out. You should also repeat this strategy periodically in order to understand if your market is changing. I have a course where I have created worksheets you can fill out in order to track and analyze this data. The best thing is, you can outsource this whole process.

CHAPTER 8

NOW FINISH YOUR ACCOUNT SETUP

SO YOU CAN GET TO THE FUN PART

It's ok if you already have an account set up, but now that you have done your research and know the content, influencers, brands, etc. that you want to focus on, you can craft your profile the right way. I am going to walk you through the steps required.

Step 1:

Make sure your username is a good one. You can change it, but better to have a good one to start than to change later (ask me how I know).

Step 2:

If you haven't done this already, you need to do it now. Set up a Facebook page for your brand or business. Very easy process.

Step 3:

Now connect your Instagram to your Facebook page so that you have a business account. The importance of this is to allow you to easily run ads and get detailed stats on Instagram about your posts. Also, it makes it easier for people to contact you.

Step 4:

Connect Instagram to your other social media accounts: Facebook, Twitter, Tumblr, Flickr, and Swarm are the main ones. This allows you to easily post to all of these when you post on Instagram. This helps extend your brand reach; it kills five birds with one stone. The main ones I recommend to being with are Facebook and Twitter.

Step 5:

Pick the ideal profile picture. You should have a really good idea what types of profile pictures to use based upon your research. The Importance of a good profile photo is that it shows that you are a legitimate account and helps people pick your account out from the lists in Instagram. You can't go wrong with a nice picture of your smiling face. But get creative and see what works best.

Step 6:

Fill out your bio completely. The goal of the bio for your business is to inform people of who you are, what you have why they should want it, and how you can help them. Don't be afraid to use emojis and include a call to action in your bio.

Step 7:

Make sure you have a link posted. You get one link on Instagram. There are a lot of strategies for what to use the link for. You should know a few based on your competitive research. I recommend having a few link options. Your main link should be used to go to an Opt-In page that gives a quick overview of your business and offers a lead magnet to get people to sign up. This is a great way to build your subscriber list for free. The next type of link you should use is for special promotions and calls to action. Say you are in real estate and you have a house you want to sell. Link to it so you can tell people to go directly there. There are a lot more examples, but the takeaway is that you need a link.

Step 8:

Put Instagram on your website and emails. You want to connect these to Instagram so people can share your content as well as visit your Instagram site. A key thing to remember, don't make it too easy for people on your website to leave and go to Instagram - why kick someone out of your store to go check out your billboard telling them to go to your store? My advice is that you put the "follow me" Instagram icon only in your website footer or on the sidebar for certain posts. For your email, only include the "share icon" unless you give people a call to action to follow you.

CHAPTER 9

FINALIZE YOUR PROFILE THEME

SHOW THE WORLD YOUR TRUE (BUSINESS) SELF

To recap, you should have all your market research done, your account set up, and ideas for what your posts and content strategies should be. This section is critical. It takes some use of your brain to get it done, but if you do it once you won't have to do it again for a while.

You need to finalize everything, write it down, and create a schedule.

Here is what you need to finalize:

Post Schedule

You need to create a schedule of posts. I recommend one to two months in advance. How many posts you need depend on you and your business. Keep in mind that the whole point of Instagram is to maximize engagement between your business and your followers. So you want to post as often as possible. I suggest at least five out of seven days a week. This is one of the fun parts. When you plan ahead and schedule your posts, you get to be creative and tell stories, link up with trends, and even start your own trends. Once you have your schedule created you can outsource everything else, except engaging with your followers via stories, direct messages comments, and likes.

Post Frequency

Now this ties into your post schedule but I am calling this out because this is the amount you post in one day. There actually isn't any harm in posting multiple times a day; in fact it can be very beneficial. Just don't post a bunch of stuff all at once. I recommend figuring out when your audience is most active and post two to three times a day. Morning, mid-day, and evening. It is up to you to determine what these posts are. So a quick heads up if you post three times a day, five days a week that will be around 60 posts a month. If you don't generate that much of your own content, this is a good setup to integrate quote posts, reposts, and crowdsourced posts.

Post Types

So if you know your themed schedule and frequency then you will know what types of posts you need to make that happen. You already know what posts work for your Instagram categories and which ones are going to be your main ones. So now just assign them to your schedule accordingly.

Tags

There are four main types of tags.

1. *Influencer tags.* These are where you tag any influencers, people, or places that show up in your photo or the person responsible for the photo. Sharing is caring and this will notify the account that you posted a photo of them.
2. *Resource Tags.* Here is where you tag the accounts that are specifically built around promoting whatever content your post is about. You should have a list. Say you post a quote, then tag a few accounts known for just posting quotes. This is put you on their radar and they may feature you for free!
3. *Location Tags.* These tags are in addition geo-tagging. I mainly use for locations. So if you take a photo in

Malibu you can tag, Malibu accounts, California, Los Angeles, etc. Same idea as resources, just with locations.
4. *Geotagging*. The goal of geotagging is to show the location of where you took the photo. This helps you show up in location based searches. It also helps you keep track of where you have been.

Captions

Again you know what types of captions to use and by now you have picked out core caption structures to assign to your post types. Write these out for each one of your posts.

Hashtags

These, which you are familiar with, help people search for your posts. They look like this "#[insertthinghere]" - literally anything can be a hashtag; it's just a keyword search. A tip is to use one or two max in your caption. These should be the most important hashtags about your photo. The reason is that your photo will be put into search feeds based on when it was posted. The feeds it gets put into are based on these hashtags. You can use Iconosquare, trending tags, keyword searches, and hashtagify.me to get the best hashtags.

> **Pro Tip**: *As soon as you post go and comment on your post with the rest of the hashtags you want to use. If you don't want people to see these hashtags, then you need five with one "." Each - no spaces, just hit "enter" after each period. You can put a max of around 30 hashtags and you should*

use at least 11, but no harm going to 30. The best way is to create hashtag lists so you can just copy and paste. This ensures your photo gets into those feeds as soon as possible.

Pro Tip2: *You should create your own hashtags for your brand. You can use these for contests or just to make it easier for people to search specifically for your brand. REI does a great job with this. They created the hashtag "#optoutside" to run contests and crowdsource images.*

Mentions

This is just when you do this "@[insert username]". I recommend only one or two of these in the photo to give credit to the top contributors of the photo. Use the tag section to call out other accounts.

So once you finalize these details you are ready to turn on your Instagram Machine. Literally. If you map all this out and schedule it, all you need to do is have someone or yourself upload all this content each day. This is why I have had you go through all the steps before so that you can outsource this. Unfortunately, at this time you can't automate the posting, but you can get reminders to post. You just created the content and instructions, so just assign someone to post for you. Then if you are a real pro, you should assign someone to monitor your analytics and let you know if things are great or if they can be improved. Then you just test.

This, my friends, is the secret formula for maximizing your Instagram account.

CHAPTER 10

SECRET GROWTH STRATEGIES
THAT MOST PEOPLE NEVER USE

Alright, you now have essentially an Instagram Machine setup. Now you need to know the best ways to consistently and quickly gain more followers. You can have the best content and strategies in the world but if no one sees it, then it doesn't matter.

I'd like to point out a very important thing about human psychology. We are natural observers and automatically gravitate and assign authority to people and things that are "well known." What makes Instagram so powerful is that it is so easy to determine what people like and what they don't like. You do this just by looking at how many followers someone has. Even if you are a well-respected brand, person, or company outside of Instagram, if you don't have a quality page and a good amount of followers this can and will negatively impact you.

Not only does it reduce your chance for your content to be spread, but it also puts you on the same playing field as people you might be trying to sell to - this is bad. In addition, there are some companies who will only do Instagram partnerships with accounts that have over a certain amount of followers. So it is your responsibility to try and get as many real followers as you can.

Pro Tip: *Do not buy followers! What I mean by this is don't pay to have someone create essentially a bunch of fake accounts to follow you just to have more followers. This is bad for two main reasons:*

1. You have a bunch of followers but they either don't exist or they don't necessarily care about your content, which leads to...
2. You risk getting the Instagram "death sentence." This is simply when you have a lot of followers but very little engagement. This shows people that you either don't understand your audience or it is fake. This impacts your credibility and brand reputation.

You should aim to have an average engagement rate (likes/followers) between 3-5% once your account gets into the thousands of followers. Anything over that and you're a rock star. If you start dipping below that, then you need to change up your strategy. (You should know the average engagement rates in your categories from your market research.)

On to the Growth Strategies:

Preload Important Content

Before you start with normal posts, it could be a good idea to incorporate a launch series of content. This could last a week or so and should have two parts:

1. Immediately upload 5-15 photos to your account before you start following a bunch of people. These photos can be calls to action, explaining what your brand is, etc. This will give new followers things to like and show them you're new and get them familiar with your brand.

2. These are your build up to launch posts. Use these once you start implementing the growth strategies. The point of these are to capitalize on your rapid follower growth. Since this will probably be the fastest growth rate of

your account, you want to try and convert as many of these followers to leads as possible.

The goal of this strategy is to get people to click on your link in your bio and convert them to leads and or customers. After your first week or two of rapid growth, you will convert things to your more stable theme. You can go back and delete these posts.

Facebook Friends

The easiest way to get followers when you start out is to follow all your Facebook friends. You can find this option in your profile tab - top left.

Contacts

In the same area as your Facebook friends you can follow your contacts.

Pro Tip: *This is a really advanced tactic for targeting all of your current contacts and even very specific ones that you want to connect with. What you do is download all your contacts from your CRM or email list or wherever and import into a Gmail account. (I recommend making a "dummy" account just for this.) Then using a "dummy" phone (so you don't have all these unnecessary contacts in your phone), upload them as contacts. Next, download the Instagram app and login to your account. Then just follow your contacts. They will be more likely to follow you back because they are familiar with you already.*

Expert Tip: *You have to check out my course, but there is a way to use LinkedIn for sophisticated targeting with this method.*

Note: *Typically on Instagram if you follow someone there is a really good chance they will follow you back. I will give you a strategy for this in minute. If you do those two tips above, you should have at least a couple hundred followers if not over 1,000 right off the bat. Also certain post types, like calls to action on temporary sales, should be deleted once the sale is over. This keeps your account looking clean and professional.*

Email List Blast

If you already have an email list, you should send out a few emails telling people to follow you on Instagram. You can be creative with how you do this, but this will help you better connect with your list as well as get people following you that already are interested in what you have to offer.

Multiple Accounts

I recommend having a business account, then having a personal account that is related to your business. What this will allow you to do is to promote your business in two places. Also, it will build your personal brand (very very important nowadays). Obviously, the content will be different. The business content and strategy is straightforward (you already outlined that) but the personal account is slightly different. However, I recommend treating it like your business account but only changing the content. If you truly want a no worries just for fun personal account to follow your buddies, then make a private account.

Expert Tip: *You can use private Instagram accounts to offer special deals and content to people that you choose. Just something to think about.*

Paid Shout outs

Getting more followers is very important on Instagram, mainly driven by everyone's egos and desire to be famous. The only reason you post something on a public Instagram account is to get validation or it's for your business. So there are accounts that turn this into a business (you can do it too). These accounts typically have a very specific theme. You should already have a list of these accounts in your categories based on your market research and should be tagging them when you post. They may feature you for free, but unless you're "Instafamous" they typically don't. For these accounts, you pay them to post a photo or photos and they tell their followers to check your account out.

Pro Tip: *I only recommend this to people who use Instagram for business. Don't pay for anything if you can't measure the return, otherwise you are wasting money. So to do a paid shout out right, you want to acquire both followers and leads. This means you need a link in your profile that leads into a sales/opt-in funnel. Your return depends on a few things. The quality of the* *shout out, your funnel setup, the amount your pay, and the amount of leads and followers you gain.*

Word of Advice: *You should test that same funnel with paid traffic from Google ads or Facebook ads first to get an idea of how it converts and the cost per lead. This ensures you have a benchmark to measure your success against and it lets you know what prices you should pay.*

Remember: *Followers aren't leads or customers, but they are essential in establishing your brand. Never pay just for followers, but don't be too concerned if the cost per lead in a paid shout out is more than the cost per lead with just Facebook ads. This is because the paid shout out helps build your perceived authority, which isn't easily measured but if done right will have positive returns.*

Long Tail Approach

Pretty much this is based on the fact that the most competition and therefore hardest area to have your "voice/content" heard/seen is where all the "top hashtags, accounts, influencers, etc. all are. If you have a million followers, you don't really notice someone with 10,000. The key concept here is that you want to keep up with the big dogs so you need to use the popular hashtags, tags, and shout out accounts, but these only make up 20 to 30% of the market. That means 70 to 80% is underserved.

Pro Tip: *Compile a list of "long tail" accounts and hashtags - these lists are separate from your "top" lists.*

Accounts

You are going to want to tag these accounts in your photos. These accounts are "small" - less than 100K followers. Now you will have to test which follower amount works best (maybe make lists for each range 1K to 10K, 10K to 30K, etc.) but some really good deals can be found with the small accounts because they want to grow. This is especially true once you get more followers than them. They are more likely to give you free shout outs or really good deals on shout outs. Plus if you make friends when they are growing, they will have your back when they get big. Depending on your business, the ratio of long tail tags vs. main tags will vary.

Hashtags

This is the same concept as the accounts. Just look for hashtags relevant to your business that aren't as popular. You can make these very specific, so that when someone searches you have significantly less competition. I'd recommend these be most of the hashtags you post in a comment instead of the caption. Don't be afraid to use the max amount (around 30).

This strategy is highly underused on Instagram. This is because everyone is focused on the top accounts and they miss out on the great returns and opportunities from the promising growing accounts."

Contests

These are a great way to drive engagement. You can send notifications for these contests out on all your platforms. You get to decide what your contest is about, but have fun and make it relevant to your business. There are a lot of tools you can use to monitor and measure contests, which I will list in the Resources section.

Reposts

These are kind of like you doing a shout out. If there are brands or people that you really like their content and it is relevant to your brand, you can repost on your page. Just make sure you give everyone the proper credit. You can always reach out to the person and ask them if you can post their content. Again you can use the long tail strategy with this.

Outreach

This is when you actively go out and like, comment, and/or follow people that aren't following you but you think would like to. You should also do this to your followers. You want to try to do this on good content. This is just a way to give. Say you have 100K followers; you could make someone's day (and possibly convert them to a loyal follower) just by liking or commenting on their posts.

Stories and Calls to Action

The great thing about the story feature is you can use it to give great content as well as another reminder or method to create a call to action. Say you post a photo and you want to really drive up the engagement, just make a call to action in your story to get people to check it out.

Pro Tip: *Snapchat, another social media platform, is almost entirely based on "stories." A lot of businesses are trying to figure out how to monetize and market on Snapchat. The Story feature on Instagram is relatively new, but it is quite possible it stole Snapchat's thunder. Because as of right now, unless you are super famous or pay for ads Snapchat is kind of isolated.*

Use both Snapchat and Instagram Stories but I'd recommend focusing on Instagram and you can always add a Snapchat Username in your profile; you'll get some followers and you can do the same calls to action.

Follow and Unfollow

This method can be dangerous and a little controversial if done incorrectly. A lot of people stress out over who follows them and who unfollows them. Personally, as a business this is something silly to worry about. Better to focus on providing great value to people who follow you through content, engagement and awesome stories. Despite people being worried about this, it is one of these best ways to continuously grow your followers. Think of it as you reaching out to say hello to someone who may could be very interested in your content but due to limiting factors (Instagram's algorithm) they haven't had a chance to see your stuff.

I am going to outline the basic tactics and if you want the advanced tactics, you will have to check out my course.

Basic Strategy: Simply go to accounts like yours (you should know these because you created lists earlier) and start following their followers.

I recommend only doing this on smaller accounts, less than 50K followers, but even around 10K or lower will be good. The reason is that the more followers you have the more diverse they will be and the higher chance they will be fake or inactive (thus lowering your rate of return on this strategy).

You want to look for accounts that have good engagement rates and lots of comments on their posts. You can actually just follow everyone that comments on a post or likes a post of one of your competitors. This ensures they are more likely to be real and active, but also they like that type of content.

Warning: *Instagram caps the amount of people you can follow in a certain amount of time (you know you have reached this when you click to follow someone and can't). Instagram also limits the amount of people you can follow in a day. Which is important because if you follow too many in one day, you will be* *temporarily blocked from following anyone. Do this too many times and your account could get shut down. That's bad. The same goes for unfollowing people. However, these count as two separate actions with different limits on each.*

A few days after you follow people (three to five days) you can start to unfollow the ones that didn't follow you back or if you don't like their content, etc.

Pro Tip: *The max amount of people you can follow is 7,500. You also want to keep in mind that if you follow too many people or have significantly less followers than you follow this will look bad on your account. If you can keep the average number of accounts you follow to under a couple 1,000, then you will look fine. This is just a rule of thumb to be decided on at your discretion.*

So my advice is to have a system that keeps the amount of people you are following consistent. Meaning if you follow 500 in a day, then you should unfollow 500 that day.

I also don't recommend going over 500 follows or unfollows each day. Also comment on and like the photos of the people you follow. This helps them by boosting their posts. This is a powerful strategy and is perfectly legitimate if done correctly, especially if the people you are following are your target market. Like I said before, you can have the best content in the world but if no one sees it then it doesn't matter. This ensures people see your content.

Automation

I am not going to go into too much detail here on automation. But I wanted to include it because it is one of the best ways to continuously grow your account without doing anything. You can automate just about everything except posts (well you can hire an employee or outsourcer for this). You can also automate posting your Instagram content to other platforms - see the Resources section for more details. Keep in mind that you should be active on your account. This means liking and commenting on people's photos genuinely. It also means posting stories and sending direct messages. A very important task that can't be automated is to make sure your posts are supporting positive comments. Delete negative comments and block accounts that may be fake or are abusing Instagram.

These are some awesome strategies that you can start using right now that will contribute to your growth. For more advanced techniques and more detailed explanations you have to check out my **Instagram Success System!**

Dylan Bradley

CHAPTER 11

BUSINESS CONTENT STRATEGIES
PUTTING IT ALL TOGETHER

The key with Instagram is to have fun, be creative, and really show people what makes you or your business awesome. I just want to outline a few content strategies you can use for your business. These are just some ideas that can help get you started promoting your business.

Day in the Life

This is a great strategy to show off your company culture. You can do this via posts or stories. You can draw people in by telling the "day in the life" story and then end the day with a call to action. A lot of fun possibilities here.

Company Milestones

Share your company milestones. Let people know that your business is doing well. It's always a good idea to promote positivity on Instagram.

Products in Action

Don't just tell people how great your offers/products are - show them! Use stories and posts to show off what your products can really do. Again, have fun and be creative.

Photo Stories

I think this is a great way to launch a new product. Just plan out what you want the final image to be then break it down into little pieces = one post each. Then post them and put hints plus calls to action in your stories and captions. Then when you post your final photo, tell people to visit your profile to see the full product.

Create your Own Hashtags

I recommend all businesses do this. It is a way to start getting your business on the minds of your followers from the start. In addition, you can use hashtags that you created to run contests. REI does a great job with this.

Sell your Photos

If you post great photos, you can actually offer them for sale. There are a lot of services out there that let you do this, but one of the popular ones is "Foap."

Exclusive Deals, Giveaways, and Promotions

Don't be afraid to offer exclusive deals to your Instagram followers. Also don't be afraid to tell people on your other social media platforms or email lists that you are only offering a deal to someone who follows you on Instagram. This can be a great way to make your current followers feel valued as well as get more people to follow you. Plus, you will get sales out of this.

Customer Features

This is one of the best things you can do. Feature your customers using your product or benefitting from your service. This shows not only that you care about and support your followers but also shows that your product/service works. When done correctly, this is like a high-powered testimonial.

Live Streaming:

This is a brand new feature and is just like Facebook Live, but the video is only available while you are streaming. This is a great way to get engagement from your Instagram followers who are on the app.

CHAPTER 12

ANALYTICS & METRICS
TURNING FOLLOWERS TO ROI

So by now you have an awesome Instagram marketing strategy. You know just about everything you need to do to get going the right way. However, one of the essential parts is analytics. If you can't measure what you are doing, then you have no idea how good or how bad it is working. I highly recommend you use a third-party analytics platform, like Iconosquare, but that's ok if you don't. Luckily for you, Instagram offers analytics when you run a business profile. You can access these through your profile tab.

Follower Growth

On Instagram it is great to have more followers. So being able to track and see how much your account grows from week to week is essential to determine how well your strategy is working. If you are doing all the things right, you can easily gain 30 or more followers a day. That would be almost 11,000 in a year. Not too bad. However, you can grow at a lot faster rates.

Ideal Post Times

This is very important because you need to use this metric to help you determine when to post during the day.

Likes on Photos

You want to get as many likes as possible on your photos. While likes don't directly equal sales, they do serve as an indicator to your followers that you have something that a lot of people like, which psychologically makes people more favorable to it. Plus it is a good metric for you to see what content your followers prefer.

Comments on Photos

While comments don't necessarily make a follower more or less interested in your posts, they are a great way for you to see how people are reacting to your posts. Also, you can see who some of your biggest supporters are. These people you will see comment a lot. You should reward them. Plus, comments are also a way you can communicate with your followers.

Engagement Rates

This is a really important metric for you to familiarize yourself with. I mentioned before that you want to get at least 3-5% engagement on your posts. With Instagram's analytics it calculates your engagement as likes plus comments. I suggest taking this number and dividing it by your total followers to see if you hit 3-5% or better. Then you can take engagement and divide it by the reach of your post. The first metric will show you how active your overall followers are. The second will show you how active the followers that saw your post are. The reason this is important is because you may have 100,000 followers, but they all won't be active or even see your post. So to get a real idea of how well it performed, you need to know how many times unique accounts saw it.

Impressions

This metric Instagram will give you. It simply is "how many times your post has been seen."

Reach

This is important for you, and luckily Instagram will give it to you. It represents how many unique accounts saw your post. This will always be lower than your Impressions.

Profile Views

Another useful stat to keep track of. This simply tracks how many people view your profile. It is good to have more, because then you have a better chance of people clicking on your link and signing up or buying something from you.

Email Clicks

Simple stat that shows how many people clicked on the email button in your profile to contact you.

Website Clicks

This is really important to pay attention to, especially if you are tracking the conversions on your landing page. This will give you an idea of how well your offer converts people from Instagram to customers or leads. Also, this metric lets you know if people are actually interested enough to click your link. Try different bio set ups or calls to action to see if you can increase this number.

Top Posts

This is a quick breakdown of which of your posts people liked the most in the past week. This is good to know so you can figure out if you should use more posts like that or fewer..

Follower Demographics

This is great for understanding your followers. It gives you the gender, age ranges for men and women, top locations for both cities and countries, as well as which days and hours your followers are most active. Knowing these things will help you ensure your messages can better connect with your followers.

There are a lot more metrics that you can look at, but you need a third-party software platform. The great thing is that all of these metrics you can get from Instagram directly in your app. I suggest recording the performance of your photos either by using a third-party system or yourself in order to really understand your account and ensure you can continuously improve and grow.

Dylan Bradley

CHAPTER 13

ADVERTISING

THE 2017 WAY TO GROW YOUR BUSINESS

Instagram is owned by Facebook. So this means if you have been advertising on Facebook, then it will be simple to start on Instagram. If not, you just need to set up a Facebook page and ad account.

I recommend doing two campaigns for the same offering - one through Facebook and one through Instagram. That way you can tell which one actually gives you a better ROI. Keep in mind that even though you want leads and sales from your Instagram campaign, you also hope to gain followers. Where on Facebook just getting sales and leads is probably your main focus. So just keep that in mind when comparing the results.

A basic overview of Instagram's ad formats:

Photo Ads

These ads look pretty much like regular photos. The main difference is that they have a "Sponsored" label on them and they also have a "Learn More" button on the bottom right corner under the photo.

Video Ads

These look just like regular video posts, but have a "Sponsored" label on the top. These can be up to 60 seconds long.

Carousel Ads

These are the exact same layout as photo ads, but they feature multiple photos that users can swipe through.

You need to keep in mind that Instagram ads should not look too "salesy." They need to be very similar to your posts. In addition, these ads will appear on the home feed. So they do need to stand out and catch the user's eye. One more thing is that most people will view these ads on their phones. So you need to ensure that your offer is very mobile-friendly.

Now you know the ad types, here are the objectives they accomplish:

- **Clicks to website:** Send people to landing pages, blog articles, or other important pages. All ad formats are supported.
- **Website conversions:** This is one of the best, and it is intended to get people to take specific actions on your website. All ad formats are supported.
- **Mobile app installs:** If you have a mobile app, then use this to get people to download it. All ad formats are supported.
- **Mobile app engagement:** Use this to drive more engagement on your mobile app. All ad formats are supported.
- **Video views:** This is great for sharing a video story on Instagram. Video Ad format is supported.
- **Reach and Frequency:** Predictable reach and greater control of how frequently your messages go out. All ad formats are supported.
- **Page Post Engagement:** This is used to get people to engage with your page. All ad formats are supported.
- **Mass Awareness:** Drive mass awareness to a large audience with a guaranteed number of impressions. All

- **Local Awareness:** Reach people locally and get them to go to your store/page. All ad formats are supported.

You will want to keep these objectives in mind when crafting your advertising. Advertising can be a very powerful tool to get results fast, and shouldn't be overlooked. However, you need to have a very specific and measurable plan and be prepared to test before launching any campaign. Also keep in mind that advertising is all about getting the best ROI, so you should have a clear idea of the results you want. If Instagram doesn't give you that, then don't advertise there. Just be smart about it and you will do just fine!

Advertising on Instagram Live

It is finally here! Instagram has joined the live video streaming game. This is very similar to Facebook Live, but on Instagram the videos are not saved for later. This is a great way to actively connect with your current followers. While you still should use Facebook Live, Instagram Live lets you deliver that same experience on the Instagram app. This is incredibly important because of how popular mobile devices are and everything is moving to mobile. You want to be ahead of the curve, right?

Since Instagram has established itself as primarily mobile, you will be able to reach people who may not tune into Facebook. This is a tremendous opportunity to efficiently reach a massive audience and deliver groundbreaking content that sets you apart from all the competition.

I want to give you an overview of how Instagram Live works. It's really easy!

Here is what Instagram Live does:

1. Share your live video with your followers, in real time. You can also share as a Direct Message to followers!
2. Watch friends' Live feeds, as well as browse the Explore tab, featuring the best live videos happening in real time.
3. You will also be able to like and comment as you watch!

The twist → All live streams disappear after they are recorded, and there are no replays. This is actually not a bad thing. It allows you to be very genuine and show the real side of you and your business. This is important because Instagram has been criticized for only showing the "perfection", which gives people a false sense of what is real and what isn't. So as a business it is going to be increasingly important to establish yourself as genuine.

Here are the very simple steps to go Live on Instagram:

1. Open your Instagram app to the "Home" Tab.

2. Click on the "story" button in the top left corner.

3. Check your surroundings, your teeth, your hair, whatever else you want because you are about to go live. Luckily it won't be saved, but you also don't get do-overs.

4. Swipe to the side so the words "live" are under the record button.

5. Start recording and sharing your content with your followers!

I told you it was easy! But the hard part, (well I think it's the fun part), is figuring out how to apply this to your business.

When done correctly, your engagement from your best users will skyrocket and assuming you aren't live streaming in the middle of the night it will only take a matter of *minutes* for your business to reach thousands of people.

Here are some strategies I recommend:

Live Showings: This would be great for real estate professionals. You know the reality TV shows about flipping houses? Have you then realized that you are living this life, but you don't have a camera crew following you? Go ahead and have your 14-year-old son or daughter film a Live walkthrough of your best property, or do it yourself and advertise your work to all your followers.

Instagram for Team Meetings/Important Presentations: This one is simple. If you want to get the message across to your team, but you are all in different places, have them watch your stream and take notes! You can dish out orders from your desk, or from an airport, depending on the business you are in.

Use Instagram Live to Pitch to Clients: You will have to be prepared ahead of time for this one, but let's imagine your industry has some tech savvy individuals that are open to new methods of communication. Invite your potential clients into your office, and create a personal connection through Instagram, instead of sending hundreds of emails.

Instagram for Job Interviews, Hiring Events, Trainings: Interesting idea here, but if you already use Skype or Google hangouts in the hiring process, you will probably get where I'm coming from. Send your potential employee a list of some tough questions, and have them respond via Instagram live stream!

Live Stream your Talents: Perhaps you are an artist of some sort, or a cook, fashion junkie, etc. You should already be using Instagram to post photos of your work. Invite followers to see your event LIVE, or simply join you for a quick cooking session, painting session, so on and so forth.

My main goal was to stir up some ideas about how Instagram can be used in the business world. Indeed, I have found myself asking the question, "why should I care about joining 500 million people who only want to stream themselves dancing live?" But since I'm an entrepreneur, always looking for opportunities to grow my business, I definitely plan to explore the business side of Instagram.

CHAPTER 14

CONCLUSION

TAKE. ACTION. NOW.

I know you are now really excited to go out and get your account started. You should do this. Take action and utilize the strategies that you have learned in this book. This was just an overview to get you started. There are a lot more in-depth strategies I teach in my Insta-Success System course. I'd love to have you join and be able to really help you get the most out of Instagram. You can sign up on my website, or just shoot me an email at "info@dylanmbradley.com".

I wish you the best of luck and I can't wait to hear about your success stories! Oh and don't forget to check out the list of resources and the special bonus section on Instagram Live. Enjoy!

Dylan Bradley

CHAPTER 15

RESOURCE SECTION

IF YOU DON'T READ ANYTHING ELSE, THIS IS YOUR SECTION

Analytic Resources:

Iconosquare: This is one of the best Instagram analytics platforms. You can track just about everything on here. In addition, you can schedule posts and Iconosquare has a great blog with lots of tips and tricks.

Hootsuite: This platform is great for keeping all your social media managed in one place.

Sprout Social: Another platform to manage all your social media.

Hashtagify.me: This resource is great to identify the best hashtags to use related to certain categories. Definitely take advantage of this when figuring out your best hashtags

SEM Rush: This tool is great for analyzing your competitors and the top businesses in your niche. You can use keyword and content info to help you figure out what hashtags and content to use and share.

Social Blue Book: Your social media accounts have value. If you want to figure out what approximately they are worth, go here. This is a great tool if you plan on using your account to get paid to post.

Social Rank: This software helps you identify your top followers on their value, engagement and a combination of those two. The best use of this is to figure out who your best followers are and then build a relationship with them.

Mention: This tool claims to be able to let you know any time your business is mentioned anywhere on the web. This allows you to respond and figure out what people are talking about regarding your business.

Keyhole: Use this tool to track and analyze any hashtag campaign you are running.

Wolfram Alpha: You can actually use this tool to analyze your Facebook profile. Since this is connected to your Instagram, you can use it to get more insights.

Rival IQ: You should use this to track the social media efforts of your competition. This allows you to see what they are doing so you can figure out if you should use a similar strategy.

Buzz Sumo: A great resource to find the most popular content for a given topic or website. This will show you not only what the top stuff is, but also it can be used to figure out a "long tail" strategy.

Automation/Outsourcing Resources:

IFTTT: This is "If This, Then That" and is a very powerful tool for linking your different social media accounts and web pages together. This allows you to post once and automatically share it elsewhere.

Zapier: Similar to IFTTT but offers more channels. However, you do have to pay for the added features. It's still a great resource.

Upwork: This is one of the best outsourcing sites. I recommend using this to find someone to manage your posts and track your analytics.

Fiverr: For all the little tasks you don't want to do go to Fiverr. Everything starts at $5, and you can get anything from Photoshop to logo design and even video creation on here.

Design Resources:

Canva: A great resource for designing your own images. It has a whole host of features, a lot of them are free, and it is fairly simple to use.

Adobe Creative Cloud: This is a subscription that gives you access to Photoshop. This is a great tool for editing your photos, videos, etc.

Click Funnels: I mentioned that you need a link in your bio. Click Funnels allows you to build landing pages customized for your business and the offer you use to get leads/customers. It is simple to use, and I highly recommend this.

VSCO Cam: This app is great for taking and editing your photos. It provides a little more editing power than Instagram's native features, and allows you to better show off the photo quality.

Instagram Apps:

Boomerang: This app integrates right into Instagram and allows you to create GIFs as content. It can be a fun way to show off some of your personality.

Layout: Sometimes you want to show more than one photo in a post. This app allows you to do that.

Hyperlapse: This is a really cool app that allows you to create time lapse posts! Plus, it also stabilizes your videos. You can have a lot of fun with this, and create some unique content!

Stock Photo Resources:

Dreamstime: Free access to photos.

Free Digital Photos: Free images, but they require you to give credit to the photographer (not always a bad thing).

Free Images: Has over 350,000 stock photos, and this database is searchable by categories.

Ancestry Images: Free image archive that features images of historical artifacts, maps, prints, etc.

BigFoto: A royalty-free photo gallery featuring a lot of photos from amateur photographers. It is organized by geographic area.

Gratisography: High-resolution images for personal and/or commercial use.

Death to the Stock Photo: Lifestyle-focused photos that are high resolution and sent to you monthly.

New Old Stock: Vintage photos from public archives without copyright restrictions.

CHAPTER 16

THE SOCIAL SECRET
SKIP THIS IF YOU ARE A "MILLENNIAL"

There is a secret to being successful on social media. I hate to disappoint you, but it is nothing new… Actually you shouldn't be disappointed, you should be very happy about this. Especially because it's a skill set that most people on social media are lacking… I say most people because the majority of people on Instagram are under 35 and fall into the category we know as "Millennials"!

For this group [read: your competition] everything is instant. I am going to say "we" because I am a part of the Millennials… So we want everything right now, and with the help of technology we can pretty much get everything right now. But as you know as well as just about every enlightened scholar, philosopher, guru, grandparent, parent… aka anyone with real life experience that the journey/process/struggle is often more valuable than the end result.

So what am I getting at? What is this secret that you already know, but are waiting for a Millennial to give to you…?

Well I am about to reveal it to you, but I just wanted to make you wait a little, because well that is the whole point.

That is the secret! Wait…

Specifically, you need to wait to make the sale. You see all of your competition is operating in a short term, in your face, constant sales mode. I agree this can work, but only short term. Remember we humans are really really really good at habituating (becoming familiar and tuning out) to situations. So what do you think is going to happen if you are constantly trying to sell? No one will listen!

They will just tune it out. So your secret weapon is not to rely on social media to sell. At least not via your profiles (do it via paid advertising). You want to rely on social media, specifically Instagram, to do the one thing that ensures a sale more than anything else…

Build a relationship with your customers!

Every great salesman knows, Shoot every great person knows, that the quality of the relationships you have with the people around you are what really contribute to your success.

So, this is how you build your Instagram or any other social media profile. Structure it to tell a story (since story telling is one of the main ways we strengthen and build relationships) and focus on building relationships with your followers. Don't even focus on selling anything via social media… in the beginning- remember "good things come to those who wait"!

So how do you actually go about building a social profile with the sole purpose of building relationships?

The simple answer is just the golden rule "treat others the way you wish to be treated".

Or a quick google search for "how to build customer relationships" yields the following (with my translation into Instagram actions):

- **Be patient in building new relationships**- don't be discouraged if you don't get a massive following overnight
- **Get to know your followers**- ask questions, look at their profiles, comment on their photos, see what they like
- **Go the extra mile**- even if it is incredibly inconvenient for you at the time- go out of your way to answer someone's question, or fix a customer service issue

- **Treat every client/follower as your most important one**- remember the golden rule. Maybe that person asking your advice with just 1 follower is actually connected to the exact person you need to radically change your business for the better? You never know.
- **Say please and thank you**- yes these matter online. So many people forget that an online interaction is still an interaction
- **Be positive**- Do you like to be around negative people? No one does, so don't go being all negative on your profile, that's one way to discourage anyone from following you.
- **Focus on what your followers/clients/customers want and not what you want them to want**- The more you can make your content show what your followers want, the more they will like it. However, don't fall into the instant gratification trap- that isn't what people really want and you're doing them and yourself a disservice by giving it to them.
- **Give genuine praise**- Comment and like your follower's content if it's genuine. Respond back to comments from your followers.
- **Actively give your attention**- Attention is the most valuable thing in the world. Typically people say this is time, but attention is more valuable because it is someone choosing to spend their time on you and just you. Don't you love when you get attention? So don't you think that your followers will love when you give them your attention?
- **Be consistent**- people are creatures of habit. So post regularly and people will begin to expect it.

- **Be empathetic**- this is encompassed by a few other points above, but it is worth stating. Empathy, the ability to understand the feelings of another, is the foundation upon which successful businesses and relationships are built. Constantly seek understanding before trying to be understood.

There are of course many other tips & tricks and I could get very specific, but I leave that up to you. I want to build a relationship with you. Ask me questions I will answer. Please tell me what you want, I will do my best to acknowledge and provide it.

Right now you have the chance to truly build a solid relationship with the people that are responsible for your future business success. You can get caught up in the hype and try to "churn and burn" through customers by repetitive and deceitful sales tactics only to make a quick buck today but have nothing to show for it in the future or you can take some time to connect with people and lay a foundation for a business set to grow over the course of the rest of your life.

Remember, that businesses may fail, they may change form, most certainly your products & services will change, but the one thing that doesn't change is you! Now, you do experience change and growth but you are still you, so why not lay the foundation of making you a very likeable you. So when someone hears your name 3 to 5 years from now and they do a quick google search or Instagram search (they will, trust me) you meet them with a friendly likable profile!

So the end result is that by using your profile to build relationships with your followers/customers/clients you eliminate all your competition. Since you are the only you- no one can compete with that. So when you go to sell it's not selling it's providing.

This is the way you win at social media. This is the way you ensure your success for years to come. This is how you build a business to last in today's world!

ABOUT THE AUTHOR

Dylan Bradley is the founder of OEQMedia, He also runs and blog and Instagram training courses at DylanMBradley.com. He got his start on Instagram in 2012. However, due to being a Division 1 Track & Field Athlete and having aspirations to get his initial start out of University at an elite consulting firm, he didn't fully join the social media game until the end of 2015.

From 2012 to 2015 He acquired the skills he needed by consulting one of the largest independent oil companies and helping them make an extra 100 million in revenue. In addition, he worked on consulting the largest oil field service company in the world and helped them design an entire organizational change program.

Once convinced he had acquired the necessary skills needed to build his own business he left his elite consulting job to be a full time Entrepreneur. Recognizing the power of Instagram, he leveraged what he had and knew to rapidly grow his Instagram account from just 400 followers in December of 2015 to over 32,100 followers by December 2016 in order to lay the foundation of his business.

He grew his account without selling a single product, running any ads or relying on the transfer of followers from any other platform. He created a system that can be applied by anyone to get noticeable results leveraging Instagram. Not only that, but the skills and resources taught in his program "Insta-Success System" can be applied to any other social media platform.

For more information about Dylan, you can check out his personal page at http://www.dylanmbradley.com/, or reach out to him on:

Instagram @dylanmbradley

Facebook @DMB0913

Twitter @DMB0913

www.ingramcontent.com/pod-product-compliance
Lightning Source LLC
Chambersburg PA
CBHW061147180526
45170CB00002B/649